BEECHAM STORIES

BEECHAM STORIES

Anecdotes, sayings and impressions of Sir Thomas Beecham

Compiled and edited by

Harold Atkins and Archie Newman

With a foreword by

Yehudi Menuhin

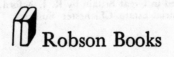
Robson Books

FIRST PUBLISHED IN GREAT BRITAIN IN 1978
BY ROBSON BOOKS LTD., 28 POLAND STREET,
LONDON W1V 3DB. COPYRIGHT © 1978 HAROLD
ATKINS AND ARCHIE NEWMAN.

First impression September 1978
Second impression November 1978
Third impression December 1978
Fourth impression March 1979
Fifth impression January 1980

British Library Cataloguing in Publication Data

Beecham stories
    1. Beecham, *Sir* Thomas, *bart.* – Anecdotes
    I. Atkins, Harold   II. Newman, Archie
    785'.092'4   ML422.B33

    ISBN   0–86051–044–1

Printed in Great Britain by R. J. Acford,
Industrial Estate, Chichester, Sussex

*To all those musicians who worked
with 'Tommy'*

Contents

Foreword

One of my most treasured possessions is a photograph of
myself (circa 15) sitting galvanised in my best blue
suit between those two unique and phenomenal figures
of English music, Sir Edward Elgar and Sir Thomas
Beecham.

On my right Sir Edward gazes with unfocussed
benevolence into the middle distance, on my left Sir
Thomas, wine glass in hand, pierces the camera's eye
with a witty dart marking the aphorism he had just
shot and which—alas!—despite all efforts I cannot
recall; alone the sound of my father's laughter rings in
my ears.

Framed by those two magnificent creatures, my look
of doltish admiration and the slightly vapid grin I offer
Sir Thomas may be forgiven, for what boy could have
been more fortunate than I, planted there discussing the
coming Albert Hall concert?

It was a revelation to me that, while remaining a
thoroughly professional musician of immense knowledge
and capacity, it was possible for a conductor to be so

elegant, so humorous, to be able to fill one with such delight and yet never lose command of either the music or the moment, or in any way diminish the seriousness of the work in hand.

It was probably my first meeting with that subtle quality, grace—a grace that he showed to his orchestra, as to his soloists—a compound of an erudition and a wit adjoined to a courtesy of heart that has now all but disappeared from daily life.

All this, and much more besides, the reader of this delightful collection will find within its pages, and he will extract from them some of that warmth and gaiety that I remember to this day.

Who said: 'Wit is folly unless a wise man hath the keeping of it'? Whoever it was would have found the epitome of his epigram in Sir Thomas Beecham.

Introduction

There are a number of books of memoirs and reminiscence of Sir Thomas Beecham, each excellent in its way,
but this is something slighter—a collection of anecdotes,
sayings and impressions. A good many are in general
circulation among musicians, but many others are little
known.

No set of stories can do justice to Beecham's wit and
humanity. A few musicians have expressed fears lest, set
down in isolation, certain stories might do him a dis-
service or appear superficial. True, we cannot always
give the complete context, or convey the casual drawl,
the emphasis on words, the mercurial love of mischief
or the waggish exaggeration. But there is so much fun,
warmth and pungency that we think it worth-while
putting these short incidents and utterances together.
Inevitably, some may have been modified by time, for
better or worse.

We are indebted to a number of friends and associates
of Beecham for their recollections, and in particular to
Mr Ronald Settle of Liverpool, Mr John Denison, former

11

director of the South Bank Concert Halls, Mr Wilfred Stiff, Mr Dennis Arundell, Mr Alfred Francis, Mr Eric Fenby and Mr Richard Arnell.

We owe thanks for permission to use short excerpts from books to William Collins Sons and Co. Ltd. (*Sir Thomas Beecham* and *Talking of Music* by Neville Cardus); Prof. Humphrey Procter-Gregg (*Sir Thomas Beecham, Conductor and Impresario*: reissued as *Beecham Remembered* by Gerald Duckworth and Co. Ltd.); Hamish Hamilton Ltd. (*The Baton and the Jackboot* by Berta Geissmar, London 1944); Victor Gollancz Ltd. (*Thomas Beecham* by Charles Reid); Hutchinson Publishing Group Ltd. (*A Mingled Chime* by Sir Thomas Beecham and *Philharmonic* by Thomas Russell); Bernard Shore (*The Orchestra Speaks*, Longmans, Green and Co. Ltd.); and John Farquharson Ltd. (*The Great Conductors* by Harold C. Schonberg, Victor Gollancz Ltd.). One or two items are taken from the Beecham Society Newsletter.

We are also grateful to EMI for permitting the reproduction of extracts from the gramophone record *Sir Thomas Beecham in Rehearsal*.

Full attributions to books and the record are listed at the end.

Our thanks are due to Mr Wilfred Stiff for casting an eye over the manuscript.

To Sir Neville Cardus, who encouraged this project, we pay our tribute, with many others, not only for setting down so many good Beecham stories, but also because this great journalist's 'sensitized plate' of a mind, as he called it, did so much to convey the wonder and intoxication of hearing great music and great orchestras.

If we have accidentally omitted acknowledgment to anyone or over-condensed someone's story, we express our regret.

H.A. and A.N.

Impressions and tributes

Neville Cardus's summing-up:
'A complex character—Falstaff, Puck and Malvolio all mixed up, each likely to overwhelm the others. Witty, then waggish, supercilious, then genial, kindly, and sometimes cruel; an artist in affectation, yet somehow always himself. Lancashire in his bones, yet a man of the world.'

♩

Shaw once said about him, with some amazement: 'Beecham is the most adult conductor I have ever met.'

♩

'I was fascinated by his personality and always touched by the friendliness and humility beneath the brilliant exterior. Remember, he always bowed first to the *orchestra* and only secondly to the audience.'—Richard Arnell, the composer

13

'It is significant that for all his affectation of disdain and his magisterial way of administering correction to bourgeoisie and hoi-polloi alike, he is known among orchestral players as "Tommy".'—Neville Cardus

ç

Sir Malcolm Sargent wrote: 'When dealing with people or circumstances, his wit so easily overcame his true feelings. We were on a Brains Trust together on one occasion, and he made a typically brilliant speech, causing tears of laughter. I replied: "Sir Thomas has made a most amusing speech—not one word of which was true!" He rose slowly to his feet and with the wicked "Beecham-twinkle" in his eye said: "I have not yet decided that it is more interesting to be truthful than amusing." '

ç

Neville Cardus wrote: 'His baton technique, often unpredictable, depended much on the watchful responses of his first desks. I have seen Beecham's baton fly from his grip high into the orchestra's empyrean. I have seen it entangled in his coat tails. In a symphonic development passage, when frequently he became impatient (if the music wasn't Mozart's), he would point his baton rapidly down to the floor of the platform, like a musical water-diviner.'

ç

A Paris tribute:
'Il devient plus italien que Toscanini, plus trépidant, plus frémissant qu'un danseur de tarantelle.'

14

After a performance of Dvořák's G Major Symphony at the Palais des Beaux Arts, Brussels, the director, Marcel Cuvelier, turned and said: 'This Sir Bichem of yours, he conducts as the bird sings!'

♩

'Sir Thomas Beecham has done more for French music abroad than any French conductor.'—Jury of the Académie du Disque Français

♩

'When Sir Thomas Beecham is rehearsing with the orchestra alone, he will go through the work to be prepared with an apparent lack of enthusiasm, sometimes in a haphazard fashion; but place *one* listener in the body of the hall, and the atmosphere changes at once. The rehearsal suddenly becomes interesting, subtle effects are obtained and the sparkle of his wit flashes like electricity.'—Thomas Russell, formerly of the London Philharmonic Orchestra

♩

Prof. H. Procter-Gregg wrote:
'Tommy often scorned his own stick, and players got what they required from something else, some movement of wrist or little finger, but mostly, as he himself said, from the eyes. "There is, you know, a certain current which passes . . . from the eyes." '

♩

'He made me feel myself to be a better player than I could possibly have been at that age, and created the impression at all times that what I was doing was exactly how and what he wanted.'—Geoffrey Gilbert, the flautist

♩

'Of course, we all play rather better for Beecham.'—Albert Sammons, the violinist

Beecham on performing

'For a fine performance only two things are absolutely necessary: the maximum of virility coupled with the maximum of delicacy.'

♩

'The grand tune is the only thing in music that the great public really understands, and flexibility is what makes it live.'

♩

'Through the whole of my career I have been looked upon as the protagonist of rapid tempi, in spite of the provable fact that in the majority of cases I have actually taken more time over performances than many of my contemporaries who have escaped entirely a similar charge.'

♩

17

To an orchestra: 'Forget about bars. Look at the phrases, please. Remember that bars are only the boxes in which the music is packed.'

At rehearsals

Sir Thomas used to repeat to his musicians the following piece of philosophical verse:

> *The world is a difficult world, indeed,*
> *And people are hard to suit,*
> *And the man who plays on the violin*
> *Is a bore to the man with the flute.*

𝄞

'After a very long experience I have discovered that the only way to have a really living and vital performance is not to rehearse it. Everyone will be listening hard to the music and that makes a great tension. I assure you it affects the public in that way too. *They don't know what's going on!* They think there is something unusual.'

'When you rehearse a work, let the orchestra play it to you. Learn it from the orchestra and then you can make your suggestions.'

♩

'Beecham didn't stop the orchestra if it made a mistake. But the second time round he did so and began to interpret the work. The third time round it was better than anybody else could do it.'—Richard Arnell

♩

Beecham called for A from the principal oboist. This player had a wide vibrato. Sir Thomas, looking round at the orchestra, said 'Gentlemen, take your pick.'

♩

'Is there a side drum? Not in this piece at all? What a pity. Very remiss of Haydn—I mean, taking the trouble to write a military symphony, limiting himself to three percussion instruments. Well, we must do something about it, I think, before we've finished with it!'

♩

At Covent Garden Sir Thomas was rehearsing with a new leader of the violins and complained 'We're not together.'
'Well, Sir Thomas,' said the new leader, 'we can't see your beat.'
'What did you say?'
The leader repeated it.
'Beat!' exclaimed Beecham. 'What do you think I am—a bloody metronome?'

To a player: 'We cannot expect you to be with us all the time, but perhaps you would be good enough to keep in touch now and again.'

♩

'Cor anglais, kindly give me some indication of your presence at four bars after letter G.'

♩

Beecham announced 'I am going to change the items this afternoon and do only Mozart.' He then pointed to the bass clarinet and remarked, 'Mr Lear, I shall not need you . . . which reminds me of an epitaph I once saw to a baby who was born at twelve o'clock and died at two minutes past. It was:

> *Seeing I was here for such a short time,*
> *It was hardly worth coming at all.*

Good afternoon, Mr Lear, and thank you very much.'

♩

To the orchestra, querulously, tapping the score: 'Nobody is playing anything like what I've got here.'

♩

At a rehearsal in the Free Trade Hall, Manchester, on a cold, foggy November morning, Sir Thomas said, 'Anybody feel disposed, on this salubrious Manchester morning, to play *In a Summer Garden* of Delius?' There was a unanimous 'No!'
'Ah, I thought not,' said Sir Thomas. He examined the scores. 'Let's see what we have here. . . . Ah, yes, the

Second Symphony of Brahms—suitable for *all* weathers, *all* seasons of the year. Come on, boys—whoops!'

♩

Once, when Sir Thomas was rehearsing an orchestra not his own, the trombones came in very loudly. He stopped and said, 'Trombones, would you please give us *forte.*'

They played even louder, and he stopped again with 'No, I'm asking for it to be played *forte.*'

They nearly burst themselves next time, but Beecham stopped again.

'I wanted *forte,*' he said mildly. 'You have been playing consistently double-*forte.*'

♩

In Beecham's earlier days there was an old cor anglais player well known for being late at rehearsals and for his repartee. One rehearsal was in full swing when he arrived wearing a very striking suit. Beecham, without stopping, said 'Good morning. I presume you have been detained by a visit to your tailor.'

'Well, not exactly, Sir Thomas,' came the reply. 'Your suit turned very nicely.'

♩

A Sibelius Festival was supported by a large list of patrons, and at a rehearsal of one of the most delicate passages of *The Death of Mélisande* one of them, a famous London hostess, burst into the hall with a clatter and a bang. Sir Thomas turned round and hissed savagely: 'My dear lady! Do you think this is Waterloo Station?'

22

Rehearsing a work with a New York orchestra made up of unemployed musicians, Beecham said to the composer, 'Mr Arnell, would you mind if I played this part of the second movement rather slower, because the poor old second bassoon can't play very well and I want to let him have a go.'

♪

'What have we got this morning?'
'The *Pathétique*, Sir Thomas.'
'Oh well, let's see what we can do to cheer it up.'

♪

'Where's that piccolo? Come right here. Forward, come on, right under the microphone and blow into it for dear life!'

♪

At a rehearsal of Verdi's *Requiem* in Queen's Hall one cold Sunday morning the 'Dies Irae' came in late. Beecham laid his stick down and called in a loud voice: 'Who is in charge of the cohort behind the platform?'
'I am, Sir Thomas,' came a voice.
'Mr ——,' said Beecham, 'a player of your experience must surely be able to render certain that the Almighty's Last Trump is executed correctly and with the requisite musicianship.'

♪

During a rehearsal of *The Bohemian Girl* the chorus off-stage missed a cue, although the chorus-master had been using the spy-hole in the backcloth (before the era of backstage television).

'Mr Robinson!' called Sir Thomas from the conductor's seat, 'what the hell do you think you're up to?'

'I don't know any more than you do,' came the voice of Mr Robinson, 'because I can't see you through the damned spy-hole!'

♩

Beecham and Jean Pougnet, the violinist, were appearing with an orchestra which seemed overawed at the rehearsal, and the start of the main piece was disastrous. Sir Thomas kept going, and after a while the players began to settle down. He leaned forward to Pougnet and said: 'Don't look now, Mr Pougnet, but I believe we're being followed.'

♩

At a rehearsal of Sibelius's Second Symphony:

'Gentlemen in the bass department, you will observe in this movement a prolonged *obbligato* passage for the contra-bass meandering through the lower reaches of the orchestra like an amiable tapeworm—may we try it?'

♩

'At Figure 19, cymbals, a grand smash of your delightful instruments to help in the general welter of sound, if you please.'

♩

One cold November morning in the old Free Trade Hall, Manchester, the intonation was appalling.

24

Beecham seemed to bear it for an abnormally long time, and then came the sniff and the inevitable pronouncement: 'It sounds like an Eisteddfod.'

ǿ

When Beecham was rehearsing with the BBC Symphony Orchestra, he noted that the violins were inclined to follow the leader, Paul Beard. He said gently, 'Look at me, not at the leader. There are two beards here. May I suggest that you pay a little more attention to *this* beard.'

ǿ

'Gentlemen in the clarinet department, how can you resist such an impassioned appeal from the second violins? Give them an answer, I beg you!'

ǿ

'I do not intend to bother about the passage at No. 6. It has never been heard yet and I doubt whether it ever will be.'

ǿ

To the orchestra at a rehearsal of Sibelius's *Lemminkainen*:
'In this piece you may find it a matter of some difficulty to keep your places. I think you might do well to imagine yourselves disporting in some hair-raising form of locomotion such as Brooklands, or a switchback railway. My advice to you is merely: hold tight and do not let yourselves fall off. I cannot guarantee to help you on again.'

Sir Thomas once stopped a rehearsal and said, 'I would like to ask the gentleman playing the big drum to be so kind as to ask the gentleman to his right, if union regulations do not preclude it, if he would be good enough to request the gentleman on *his* right, who is holding the cymbal, to *hit the damned thing a bit harder!*'

On orchestras

'There are two golden rules for an orchestra: start together and finish together. The public doesn't give a damn what goes on in between.'

♩

When Sir Thomas had not appeared at 1.25 p.m. for a lunch at 1 o'clock in Liverpool, the Lord Mayor ordered it to be served without him, and when he did appear said irately, 'You're late!'

Beecham quelled him with a look and replied: 'You ought to be grateful I've got here at all. I've been trying to put your orchestra into some sort of shape for tonight's concert. By rights it would take three years—not three hours!'

♩

Discussing a very cosmopolitan American orchestra he had conducted, Sir Thomas said: 'There are all races—

the first flute is French, the oboe Italian, the clarinet Dutch, and the bassoon a Chinaman. They have not really got a language in common, and it was only possible to communicate with them by cabbalistic signs and symbols, as with the Cannibal Islanders!'

♩

Beecham once said to Richard Arnell: 'I don't believe the orchestra as we know it will survive. I think the future lies with the chamber orchestra of highly professional soloists.'

Reactions to audiences

'The English may not like music, but they absolutely love the noise it makes.'

♀

'One of the drawbacks of opera in English, where everything that is sung or said can be instantly understood, is that our public, which has a lively sense of humour, never misses an opening for a laugh.'

♀

To an audience:
'Ladies and gentlemen, in upwards of fifty years of concert-giving before the public, it has seldom been my good fortune to find the programme correctly printed. Tonight is no exception to the rule, and therefore, with your kind permission, we will now play you the piece which you think you have just heard. ...'

He told the concert-goers of one provincial city that they looked as if they had lived on grass for three years, like the king in the Bible. On the whole he would prefer to conduct for people in deepest Africa who beat tom-toms and lived on nuts.

♪

Once at Covent Garden during a performance of *Fidelio* Beecham suddenly turned round to the stalls and shouted 'Stop talking!' Later, at ill-timed applause from the gallery, he went further, crying out 'Shut up, you!'

♪

An audience once greeted Beecham with complete silence. He glanced at it for a moment, then turned to the orchestra and said: 'Let us pray.'

Working with players

Describing a disastrous lapse of memory by Alfred Cortot during a piano concerto he was conducting, Beecham declared: 'We started with the Beethoven, and I kept up with Cortot through the Grieg, Schumann, Bach and Tchaikovsky, and then he hit on one I didn't know, so I stopped dead.'

♩

Vladimir de Pachmann stopped playing in the second movement of Chopin's Second Piano Concerto and said to Sir Thomas, who was conducting:
'Isn't it lofly?'
Beecham replied, 'It is indeed lovely, Mr Pachmann, but would you mind carrying on?'

♩

Beecham decided at Leeds Town Hall that for Vaughan Williams's *Pastoral* Symphony, which ends with an unaccompanied soprano solo at a distance and a prolonged trumpet solo, he would give a more romantically remote effect by having both in the gallery. He said to Ernest Hall, the trumpet player: 'Would you oblige me by ascending to that arcade at the top of the building, where you will find a charming young lady. Try not to pay too much attention to the young lady, but keep in what touch you can with us.'

♩

Discussing the acquisition of certain players for his new orchestra, Beecham was asked: 'Do you think they will come?'

He replied, 'I am certain, and for a very good reason. They are *bored to death* where they are.'

♩

Starting up Berlioz's *Trojan March* in Paris: 'Come on, brass, give 'em hell!'

♩

A woman pianist and Beecham were not getting on in a Mozart concerto. He conducted in an uninterested way, and her playing left a lot to be desired. At the interval the librarian went in to see Sir Thomas and asked, 'Shall we leave the piano on or take it off?'

Beecham thought for a moment and then said, 'Oh, leave it on. Anyway, it will probably slink off by itself.'

♩

For a performance of Debussy's *La Mer* the Liverpool Philharmonic Orchestra engaged a North Country

Caricature by Emu

Portrait by Gordon Anthony

occasional contra-bassoonist whose sound was not to everyone's taste. When this player could not attend the first rehearsal, Beecham was enraged. But, calming down on entering the rehearsal hall, he remarked to the manager: 'It'll be a little hard on the mind, but perhaps it will be easier on the ear.'

♩

After playing the *Prince Igor* Polovtsian Dances rather fast one night during a Diaghilev ballet season, Beecham leaned down to the leader of the orchestra and said, 'We made the b——s hop, what?'

♩

To a woman cellist sawing away in an Australian orchestra: 'I wonder, madam, if you would try to take the music not quite so much *to heart*.'

Attitudes to instruments

Beecham gave the following definitions:

The organ: 'A mechanical box of whistles.'

The harpsichord: 'Sounds like two skeletons copulating on a corrugated tin roof.' 'A birdcage played with a toasting-fork.'

The trombone: 'A sluice pump.'

The upright piano: 'A musical growth found adhering to the walls of most semi-detached houses in the provinces.'

𝄞

Sir Thomas was staying at a rented house near Glyndebourne, when he was most disturbed one morning by a loud cacophony of bugles, other brass instruments and drums emanating from the nearby village green. It was the band of the local Boys' Brigade, and Sir Thomas suggested that it should play a little farther off.

'You know what's the trouble with you, sir,' the youthful leader said.

'And what is the trouble with me?' asked Sir Thomas. 'You just don't appreciate good music.'

♩

To a trombone player: 'Are you producing as much sound as possible from that quaint and antique drainage system which you are applying to your face?'

♩

A musician playing the tuba made a deep shake on the wrong note. Beecham said 'Thank you, and now would you pull the chain?'

♩

A woman confided to Sir Thomas that her son wanted to learn an instrument, but she couldn't bear the purgatory of his practising in the initial stages. 'What is the best instrument?' she asked.

'I have no hesitation, madam,' he said, 'in saying the bagpipes. They sound exactly the same when you have finished learning them as when you start learning them.'

Encounters with singers

When Sir Thomas was rehearsing Massenet's opera *Don Quichotte* with Chaliapin as Don Quixote, the voice of Dulcinea twice came in too late as the Don died. Beecham said to the soprano, 'Twice has Mr Chaliapin died in bed, with the most affecting realism, and twice you have sung too late. Why?'

'It's not my fault, Sir Thomas,' replied the soprano in panic. 'It's—it's Mr Chaliapin. He dies too soon.'

'My dear,' said Beecham, 'no opera singer ever dies too soon!'

𝄡

'Many years ago, when I told the gallery to shut up in the middle of an opera, there was no applause for three weeks afterwards. The Italian tenors all wanted to go home, because they couldn't get a hand for anything.'

36

Asked by Sir Thomas to sing the soprano part in Handel's *Messiah*, a singer confessed that she did not know the oratorio, but accepted the offer. Meeting her some time later, he asked how the task of learning the part was progressing.

'I've been working hard on it,' she replied. 'The score goes with me *everywhere*—to work, to meals, up to bed at night. . . .'

'Then', he replied, 'may I trust we may look forward to an immaculate conception . . . ?'

♩

Once, when auditioning a baritone for *Carmen*, Sir Thomas remarked, 'He's made a mistake—he thinks he's the bull instead of the toreador.'

♩

Of one *Walküre* soprano Beecham said her singing reminded him of a cart coming downhill with the brake on.

♩

When Ezio Pinza, the most famous Don Giovanni of the 1930s, came on for rehearsal one day at Covent Garden, he was dressed unnecessarily in a rather elaborate costume as the Don. Sir Thomas stopped and cried out: 'Good God, man, where did you get those clothes?—Portobello Road?'

♩

A soprano was rehearsing the dying Mimi in the last act of *La Bohème* with Beecham conducting. He called out: 'I want more tone—I can't hear you.'

'Don't you realise', she protested, 'that one can't give of one's best when one is in a prone position?'
'I seem to recollect', he replied, 'that I have given some of my best performances in that position.'

Moments in opera

'Opera is the most highly developed and complete form of art in music, and to sing in opera should be the aim of every vocalist. All vocal performance should be dramatised and opera should be the goal of every composer. And the utility of concerts should be to train audiences and all concerned for opera.'

♩

'The British genius for opera, if there is one, should be devoted to comedy.'

♩

At the dress rehearsal of *Götterdämmerung* everything went wrong on the stage. The scenery was not ready. The lighting was not correct. The Siegfried had refused to come to the rehearsal on some pretext. Sir Thomas walked about the stage, roaring like a caged lion. The atmosphere was at white heat. The orchestra, in their pit, sensed the tension, and relieved the situation by striking up *The Blue Danube*.

Sir Thomas, ever at one with his orchestra, responded at once and rushed down to the pit. Taking up his baton, he conducted *The Blue Danube* at full Wagnerian strength, tubas included. The stage was nonplussed for the moment. The German prompter, making for his box, was heard to mutter, 'In Dresden this would be absolutely impossible.'

♩

Douglas Steele wrote of an afternoon with Beecham at Covent Garden:

'He said, "I want you to turn over for this terrible piece." He went to the upright piano and the "terrible piece" was *Götterdämmerung*. As fast as he roared, coughed, cursed, sang (and what singing!), I turned. When I missed a turn, he cursed, not me but the *Ring*. "Damn awful thing, what? Barbarian lot of Nazi thugs, aren't they?" The following evening he gave an absolutely majestic performance of the work.'

♩

During a rehearsal of the colloquy between Brünnhilde and Wotan in the second act of *Die Walküre*, with two great personalities on the stage, Frida Leider and Rudolf Bockelmann, Sir Thomas puffed expostulatingly and exclaimed: 'Isn't Wagner an old bore!'

♩

One day the rehearsal had been long and strenuous: the orchestra and Sir Thomas had worked indefatigably at some great passage of Wagner. At last Sir Thomas took out his watch:

'My God!' he said, 'we have been playing for two solid hours and we're playing this bloody tune still!'

♎

Emphasising the importance of scenery, he said: 'I once notified the manager of the theatre of, I think, King's Lynn, where *Tristan* was being put on, what scenery was needed. For the second act a tower was required. I had no time before the performance to inspect the scenery, and you may judge of my astonishment, when the curtain rose, to discover none other than our old friend the set for the second act of *Iolanthe*, with Big Ben in the background.'

♎

There was trouble over the designer for Beecham's revival of *The Bohemian Girl* and he rejected several names at a meeting at Covent Garden. After about two hours David Webster, the administrator, said 'Well, Sir Thomas, have *you* anybody to suggest?'

'How is Aubrey Hammond these days?' Beecham asked.

Webster, observing that Beecham did not know he was dead, replied tactfully (or perhaps mischievously), 'He is as well as can be expected.'

'Well, ring him up,' said Beecham, with some asperity.

Webster replied: 'Sir Thomas, I don't think he would care to be disturbed.'

♎

Beecham stopped a rehearsal of *Die Meistersinger* to

41

ask the tenor singing Walther: 'Do you consider yours is a suitable way of making love to Eva?'

'Well, there are different ways of making love, Sir Thomas,' replied the tenor.

'Observing your grave, deliberate motions,' said Sir Thomas, 'I was reminded of that estimable quadruped, the hedgehog.'

♩

Telephoning for the eighth time about a rehearsal for an opera, Beecham gave the festival director a good lambasting which lasted a long time.

He finished: 'And my last comment is this. . . .' There was then the sound of tearing paper.

'What was that, Sir Thomas?' asked the director.

'I was just tearing up my contract.'

'You're mistaken,' said the director. 'You never had one.'

They finished the day with an excellent dinner.

♩

The BBC had an agreement with the Covent Garden Opera Syndicate to broadcast any opera on certain terms. When *The Bohemian Girl* was presented in the Festival of Britain, the presumption that it was covered by the agreement was mistaken.

Beecham came in front of the curtain after one performance and said to the audience: 'Ladies and gentlemen, you may have read in a certain magazine, which is, I believe, called the *Radio Times*, that this opera is to be broadcast. All I can say is that Mr Arundell and myself have been offered only £25 each. It will not be broadcast.'

It was in fact broadcast as announced after suitable readjustments had been made.

At an early Covent Garden performance of *Elektra* Beecham was heard telling the orchestra: 'The singers think they're going to be heard, and I'm going to make jolly well certain that they are not.'

♀

Some of Dame Ethel Smyth's influential friends persuaded Edward VII to attend the first night of her opera *The Wreckers*, which Beecham had put on.

Sir Thomas said he afterwards asked the Private Secretary, out of curiosity, what the King thought about it.

'I don't know,' was the reply.

'I said "He must have said something." "Yes," said the Private Secretary, "He said something. Three-quarters of the way through he woke up suddenly and said, 'Fritz, that's the fourth time that infernal noise has roused me. . . .'"''

♀

Beecham was rehearsing *Die Meistersinger* in Cologne and the orchestra was not being particularly co-operative. Beecham whispered over his shoulder to Dennis Arundell, 'I don't suppose it matters—it's only a gala performance.'

There was almost antagonism between him and the players during the last scene, and when the leader asked three times in one passage for the four beats in the bar which they were used to instead of two, Beecham replied: 'I don't care what they're used to: they're getting two.'

At the performance, however, after an overture that was disastrous because unrehearsed, Beecham won everybody over as the opera progressed, until in the last scene singers, orchestra and audience were completely

43

under his spell. His solo curtain-call lasted for more than twenty minutes.

♩

Beecham was conducting the rehearsal of an English opera. The composer intervened occasionally with such remarks as 'Sir Thomas, I would suggest a change here' or 'Could you do this . . .?'
Each time Beecham turned to his orchestra with the words: 'The same again, gentlemen, please.'

♩

There was a break in the recording session of an opera in the Kingsway Hall. Sir Thomas was alone, except for a violinist replacing a broken string. Some recording engineers and orchestral officials entered and one asked how things were progressing.
'Reasonably well,' said Sir Thomas. 'But I sometimes long for the days of the old castrati. You knew where you were with them.'

♩

After Neville Cardus had complained that Beecham had ruined a performance of *Siegfried* by too speedy a tempo in the last act, Sir Thomas said: 'You critics are very inhumane. My orchestra had been in the pit on a hot summer night since 5.30. At the beginning of the last act I took note of the time—after 10 o'clock. And the pubs about to close at 11!
'My orchestra had not had a drink for hours. And many of the dear people in my audience had to get back home to Woking and Pinner. So I said to my orchestra "Whoops!" . . .'

On French lyric opera:
'I would give the whole of Bach's Brandenburg Concertos for Massenet's *Manon* and would think I had vastly profited by the exchange.'

ѣ

At Covent Garden:
'His lunch was sent in from Boulestin's and was a bright, and often brilliant, interruption in the day's routine. Enough was always provided for the many interesting people who dropped in. . . . At rehearsals Sir Thomas was a living dynamo. Everything depended on his inexhaustible energy, and it seemed that there was no side of the work which he could safely delegate to anyone else. To spare his voice he used a police whistle which hung round his neck on a black ribbon.'

ѣ

The stage staff were taking rather long over a quick-change scene at a Covent Garden opera dress rehearsal and David Webster asked the producer, Dennis Arundell, not to trouble about all the scenery as Sir Thomas, in front of the curtain, would be getting angry.

As this was the only chance they had of setting up the scenery, Arundell carried on, declining to bother whether Beecham was angry or not.

After a while they heard a bellow from the other side of the curtain: 'Gentlemen, this is very boring. Let us play something. What about *The Blue Danube*? Ta-*ra*-ra-*ra*, ra-ra ra-ra!'

ѣ

When an orchestra of Wagnerian dimensions over-flowed into the stage boxes at Drury Lane during

45

the rehearsal of an elaborate home-produced opera, Beecham stopped during a deafening *tutti* and said to the percussionists: 'Gentlemen in the box, you are making an entirely inadequate din. Kindly play twenty times as loud.'

♩

During the First World War:
'The addition of *Tannhäuser* and *Die Walküre* to the repertoire provoked the ire of a certain newspaper magnate, who liked to think of himself as the real ruler of England and the keeper of all men's consciences. In his view German music was an integral part of the German soul. . . . I really ought, he urged, to banish it from my theatre; otherwise he would have to launch the thunderbolt of disapproval against me in his columns. . . .

'I knew he had some fine old German pictures in his house of which he was justifiably proud, and I undertook, if he would bring them into Trafalgar Square (having well advertised the event a week ahead in all his journals) and burn them in full view of the public as a protest against the abysmal iniquity of the Teutonic spirit, that the very next day I would withdraw everything of Wagner from my programme. . . . He was so bowled out by the proposition that for quite half a minute he was silent. Then the suspicion of a smile appeared on his face which by and by broadened into a grin, and he at last said: "It is rather silly, isn't it?" And there we left the matter.'

♩

'A very old gentleman whom I hadn't seen for a long time said to me, "You know, as far back as 1910 I went to a rehearsal of yours at Covent Garden of

Salome and I remember very well that at a certain moment you stopped and said 'Where is the prophet?' I have been wondering all this time whether you were referring to somebody on the stage or the financial condition of the company."

'I said "*Both!*" '

𝄞

To Klemperer during an apathetic rehearsal of *Carmen* at the Metropolitan Opera House, New York: 'I must bring electricity into this lazy body.'

Attitudes to composers

Mozart:
'He emancipated music from the bonds of a formal age, while remaining the true voice of the 18th century. His new sentiment or emotion, as expressed by a matchless technique, was his supreme gift to the world. That sentiment was an intimacy, a masculine tenderness, unique—something confiding, affectionate.'

♩

'If I were a dictator I should make it compulsory for every member of the population between the ages of four and eighty to listen to Mozart for at least one-quarter of an hour daily for the coming five years.'

♩

When at the lunch on his seventieth birthday telegrams were read, amid applause, from notable people in various parts of the world—including composers such as Strauss, Sibelius and Stravinsky—Beecham waited till the applause had died down and then inquired gently: 'Nothing from Mozart?'

48

Beethoven:
'The best of Beethoven's music, excepting the first four of his piano concertos, and the third, fourth and sixth of his symphonies, is second-rate, measured by values set up by Mozart.'

♩

Of the third movement of Beethoven's Seventh Symphony Beecham demanded: 'What can you do with it?—it's like a lot of yaks jumping about.'

♩

'Even Beethoven thumped the tub; the Ninth Symphony was composed by a kind of Mr Gladstone of music.'

♩

'I was going to do Beethoven's Mass in Edinburgh,' Beecham once told Richard Arnell, 'but I understand that the Queen is going and the Moderator will not allow a mass to be done in front of her. So I'm going to do Beethoven's Ninth instead—very poorly orchestrated, but I've done my best with it.'

♩

Bach:
'Too much counterpoint—and what is worse, Protestant counterpoint.'

♩

Brahms:
'That old bore.'

49

Rossini:
After a performance of the Overture to *William Tell*
at a spanking pace at the St George's Hall, Liverpool,
Sir Thomas said to a friend: 'That quite zipped along,
didn't it? I don't think Rossini intended it to go that
fast, but I think the old boy would have liked it like
that, don't you?'

♩

'It took him a full session of three hours to record to
his satisfaction the first four minutes of the *William Tell*
Overture. The recording company secretly fumed at such
profligacy; Sir Thomas characteristically rewarded the
individual achievements of the five solo cellists and
remedied their nervous exhaustion with champagne.'

♩

Wagner:
'A genius, no doubt; but too often excessively theat-
rical and emotional. *Lohengrin* was his only stylish work
—the Germans have no idea of style.'

♩

Asked whether he once cared less about Wagner than
he now did, he replied 'That is impossible.'

♩

Bruckner:
After conducting the Seventh Symphony he said of
Bruckner's organizational style: 'In the first movement
alone I took note of six pregnancies and at least four
miscarriages.'

Delius:

When Eric Fenby, Delius's amanuensis, asked Beecham what it was that had first attracted him about Delius's music, he replied: 'Here was a composer whom I had never seen or heard of before; whose music was unlike any other, or anything that was being written at the time: that was about 1907. Nobody seemed to know what the devil to make of it! I found it as alluring as a wayward woman and determined to tame it. . . . And it wasn't done in a day.'

♩

Beecham was rehearsing *A Mass of Life* in Delius's presence. As usual Sir Thomas was not using a score, and at one point Delius indicated by a small gesture that Beecham was not correct. Someone was sent to another part of London to fetch the original score and on his return Beecham was proved right. Proceeding with the rehearsal, he remarked: 'Frederick, my dear boy, I do wish you could remember your music as well as I do!'

♩

'I have observed that you never give a first performance of Delius,' Eric Fenby said to Beecham.

'No,' was the reply. 'I always let somebody else make a damned fool of himself with the music and then I come along later and show how it's got to be done.'

♩

Conducting a broadcast concert for the BBC at the Kingsway Hall, Sir Thomas announced: 'We will now have the Second Dance Rhapsody of Frederick Delius,

51

a work which was given some years ago and of which we shall now hear the first performance.'

𝄩

Elgar:
Though not an Elgar man, Beecham once declared that nobody had written an original tune since Elgar and added that *Land of Hope and Glory* was a splendid one.

𝄩

Description of Elgar's A flat Symphony: 'The musical equivalent of St Pancras Station.'

𝄩

Beecham was telling Neville Cardus about his musical plans for the season and Cardus kept asking 'What about Elgar?'
Beecham continued to mention other composers he had picked. 'But what about Elgar?' Cardus kept repeating.
At last Beecham said: 'What about him? Isn't he well?'

𝄩

Britten:
'The only English composer worth while that has emanated from one of our colleges of music.'

𝄩

Stravinsky:
'There is behind his façade of ingenious notes and

patterns no continuous personality. . . . I do not find in Stravinsky's newest productions convincing signs that he has arrived at wisdom, even yet.'

ǫ

Schoenberg:
'For me, much of Schoenberg is unintelligible, and remains unintelligible, much as I study his scores.'

ǫ

Vaughan Williams:
Beecham did not care for the music of Vaughan Williams. When someone said to him, 'Surely you wouldn't write off that wonderful *Fantasia on a Theme by Thomas Tallis*?' he replied: 'No, but Vaughan Williams made the cardinal error of not including in all his compositions a theme by Tallis.'

ǫ

Having to conduct a Vaughan Williams symphony, he seemed to do little more than beat time to it at a rehearsal. He was still beating time when he suddenly discovered that the orchestra was silent.
'Why aren't you playing?' he asked mildly.
'It's finished, Sir Thomas,' said the leader.
He looked down, turned the page over, found it empty and said 'So it is. Thank God!'

ǫ

At the end of Vaughan Williams's *Pastoral* Symphony in the BBC's Maida Vale studios, before the announcer could say 'You have been listening to . . . ', Beecham leaned over the rostrum to the man playing the celeste and remarked: 'A city life for me!'

53

On himself

'I am generally admired and rendered notorious for all sorts of doubtful qualities and doings, but I never receive recognition of the one gift which I command beyond any other—my gift for industry, patient industry.'

§

'I have always been noted for my instability. I am a very, very low-brow.'

§

'I am not the greatest conductor in this country. On the other hand I'm better than any damned foreigner.'

§

'My father nourished a passion for musical-boxes of every description, and the house almost overflowed with them. . . . The visitor who hung up his hat on a certain

54

peg of the hall rack, or who absent-mindedly abstracted the wrong umbrella from the stand, would be startled at having provoked into life the cheerful strains of *William Tell* or *Fra Diavolo*. But others were serious and solid affairs, elaborate of build, full of strange devices ... how I loved them then, and how I lament their absence now!'

♩

'Prompted more by the urgings of one of my form-masters than by any overpowering aesthetic impulse, I let myself in for playing the big drum in a military band. Rossall was the first school in the country to found a Cadet Corps and to practise all the operations and manœuvres of a miniature army; and my chief recollection of this quasi-patriotic effort was tramping up and down the country on what seemed like endless and fruitless quests, clad in a tight and ill-fitting uniform and burdened with a gigantic object which every five minutes I longed to heave into the nearest ditch.'

♩

Beecham left Oxford after only eighteen months, by his own desire. Years later he hazarded the opinion that the Warden of Wadham had been sorry to lose him, though he had remarked: 'Your untimely departure has perhaps spared us the necessity of asking you to go.'

♩

His own description of his peculiar singing:
'One thing no one will give me the slightest credit for is doing any *work*. ... But I do, on my own, of course. ... I sit down quietly over my orchestral score and sing

55

all the parts through, one after the other. . . . My powers of voice-production leave something to be desired, but I can make some sort of onomatopoeic reference to the various instruments . . . and so I sing all through their parts. And if I cannot sing a work, I cannot conduct it.'

♩

Sir Thomas was repeatedly whistling a passage from a Mozart concerto in a New York taxi and his exasperated companion exclaimed at last: 'Must you do that?' Sir Thomas replied calmly, 'You, my dear fellow, can only hear my whistling: I can hear the full orchestra.'

♩

He said to a young musician after tea at the Midland Hotel, Manchester: 'I'm going to throw you out now.'
'Are you having a sleep before the concert?' asked the young man.
'Certainly not. I'm going to look at my scores.'
'But you always conduct from memory.'
'It is because I'm going to throw you out that I can look at my scores so that I *can* conduct them from memory.'

♩

'I don't know how many friends I have. I have a title, money—when I'm not losing it in opera ventures—and eminence in the world of music. If I lost my eminence and my money and my title, I wonder how many I should have. That I shall never know.'

Of his insolvency

Excusing himself for a sudden departure from a rehearsal he was conducting, Sir Thomas said: 'I understand there is someone to see me from the Official Receiver's office. . . . And for what he is about to receive may the Lord make him truly thankful.'

♩

A banker, mystified by the complications of the Covent Garden estate, which caused bankruptcy proceedings to be taken against Sir Thomas in 1920, stopped him in the street and asked, 'Do you owe, or are you owed, two million pounds?' He replied: 'The answer is in the affirmative . . . in both cases.'

♩

'His amazing library of scores was available to me in the small room through which he used to shoot at top speed to evade, among others, two tiresome people who were, I think, his accountants, and he invariably tried to give them the slip by the exit from his music library which led into the Opera House circle. He trained me to let them bang and shout at the outer door, "Open up! Open up!" and when I judged the banging to have gained Sir Thomas enough time, I would open up. Then they shouted, "Where is he? Where's the old boy gone?" '—Reminiscence of Douglas Steele

On other conductors

Foreign conductors:
'Why do we in England engage at our concerts so many third-rate continental conductors when we have so many second-rate ones of our own?'

ℚ

Furtwängler:
'Although Sir Thomas had the greatest regard for Furtwängler as an artist, he adopted a paternal attitude towards him and generally addressed him as "my boy".
... He was always very kind and when Furtwängler used to come up and peep through the door, he would call out cheerily: "What can I do for you, my lad?" '

ℚ

Richter:
'All these damned foreign importations! Take Richter He could conduct five works, no more.'

Strauss:
'It is not known in this country that the most accomplished conductor since Nikisch was Richard Strauss—when he was in the right mood.'

♩

Toscanini:
'Talking of Toscanini, I hear he is in some trouble with his eyes and has therefore to conduct from memory. . . . I am sorry to hear it. . . . indeed a *double affliction* when you consider how many years he has been *practically* tone-deaf.'

On another occasion: 'A glorified Italian bandmaster.'

♩

Sargent:
When Beecham, who knew of Sir Malcolm Sargent's nickname 'Flash Harry' (derived from a broadcast*), heard that he was conducting concerts in Tokyo, he remarked 'Ah!—Flash in Japan.'

♩

Beecham and Sargent were on good terms and Sargent did not mind such little pleasantries as the comment when he returned from a visit to the Middle East. He told Sir Thomas that he had been detained and then released by the Arabs.

'Released?' exclaimed Sir Thomas. 'Had they heard you play?'

* The name was said to have originated in a radio announcer's remark, when Sargent had just appeared in the BBC Brains Trust, that the programme was going over to a concert conducted by him 'like a flash.'

A propos of a story that Sir Malcolm Sargent had been kidnapped in China, Beecham said 'My dear fellow, I had no idea the Chinese were so musical.'

♩

Another Sargent story refers to the time when he had just received a knighthood. Beecham was being told that another conductor played the National Anthem more quickly than he did. He asked 'Who is it?'
'Sir Malcolm Sargent.'
'I didn't know he'd been knighted,' said Beecham. 'I knew he'd been doctored.'

♩

Von Karajan:
'A kind of musical Malcolm Sargent.'

♩

Barbirolli:
'Barbirolli has worked wonders with the Hallé. He has transformed it into the finest chamber orchestra in the country.'

♩

Cantelli:
Emerging from the lift at the Royal Festival Hall, Beecham encountered a rising and very elegant young conductor about to go up. Also getting into the lift was a small and insignificant-looking man. Someone said, 'Allow me to introduce Mr Guido Cantelli.'
'How are you? I'm glad to meet you,' said Sir Thomas, cordially shaking hands with the small and insignificant-looking man.

On British music

After conducting a concert in a festival of English music, Sir Thomas remarked: 'Well, I think we have successfully paved the way this afternoon for another quarter of a century of German music!'

§

Commissioning a work, *Landscapes and Figures*, Sir Thomas said to Richard Arnell: 'Not a symphony—there are too many English symphonies this year, or any year. Write me a work like a string of pearls that will show off my orchestra.'

§

'British music is in a state of perpetual promise. It might almost be said to be one long promissory note.'

The musical profession

'This is the only country in the world where musicians are not expected to live like ordinary people. It is a tradition here that composers and most instrumentalists have always starved, and as we are a sentimental people we think that this tradition should be upheld.'

♩

When a promised payment for extra services was not received by LPO players, one of them brought it to Beecham's notice. Sir Thomas said, 'I will assist you to indite a letter to Mr Harold Holt' (then managing the orchestra). This was done, and after a long delay an evasive and imprecise reply was received, but no money.

After Holt had ceased to manage the orchestra, a player recalled the matter to him at a party. Holt said: 'Tell me, who helped you to write that very forcible letter to me?' The player admitted that it was Beecham, and Holt laughed heartily.

'Why so funny?' asked the player.

Holt replied: 'Because he drafted my letter back to you.'

♩

Sir Thomas once described a distinguished orchestra as 'this collection of disappointed soloists', referring to the fact that the training offered by schools of music had been primarily directed towards producing soloists.

♩

When shown an inscription in a Sussex graveyard saying 'Here lies a fine musician and a great organist', Sir Thomas remarked: 'How on earth did they get them both into so small a grave?'

Rehearsing: with the London Philharmonic Orchestra in 1944 (above), *and with the Royal Philharmonic Orchestra in 1958* (below)

The 15-year-old Yehudi Menuhin with Beecham and Sir Edward Elgar in 1932

Sir Thomas with Harold Atkins and John Pennington, first leader of the Royal Philharmonic Orchestra, in London, 1946

On concert halls

Of the Royal Albert Hall (and its famous echo): 'British composers should all endeavour to have their works performed in this hall; they will thus be assured of at least two performances.'

♩

To Clifford Curzon, after a Beethoven piano concerto: 'You did play the last chord of that cadenza, didn't you?'
'No, you never gave me time.'
'Oh, I thought I heard it. It must have been the echo of this confounded Albert Hall.'

♩

An early impression of the Royal Festival Hall (modified later): 'Like a disused mining shack in Nevada. Frivolous and acoustically imperfect.'
Another time: 'An inflated chicken coop.'

On the BBC and broadcasting

To a young friend looking for a BBC job: 'What on earth do you want to get on the BBC for? London is divided into two sections musically. One wants to get into the BBC and the other wants to get out, and I find it strangely reminiscent of modern matrimony.'

ℓ

'Broadcasting is this world's greatest misfortune.'

ℓ

The BBC: 'A monopolistic piece of lunacy.'

ℓ

Television: 'Three-quarters of television is for half-wits. The boxing's all right.'

On critics and academics

'Criticism of the arts in London, taken by and large, ends in a display of suburban omniscience which sees no further than into the next-door garden.'

♩

'The trouble with music critics is that so often they have the score in their hands and not in their heads.'

♩

'I have carefully noted, over a period of nearly a year, the London critics' printed opinions of Schoenberg, Berg, Webern and Stravinsky, and not once have I read a word of really adverse judgment of any of them, not one word. Apparently these composers cannot go wrong.'

♩

To a music critic: 'You know, my dear fellow, you

belong to a fraternity that has almost a genius for stating what is exactly opposite to the true facts.'

Members of the Delius Trust were once discussing the setting up of a university professorship of music. Someone suggested a chair of musical criticism.

Sir Thomas observed: 'If there is to be a chair for critics, I think it had better be an electric chair.'

'A musicologist is a man who can read music but can't hear it.'

'Doctors of Music! That means they have sat on their bottoms for six hours and done a paper on harmony, but they can't play the National Anthem.'

On America

'As for any real culture, it will take them fifty years
to discover what the word means, and probably another
fifty to absorb what Europe has had to bequeath to them
in that respect.'

♭

The telephone rang in Sir Thomas's hotel room in
New York and a voice with a strong American accent
said, 'Is that you, Sir Tammas Beech'm?' 'Speaking,'
said Sir Thomas. 'Who is that?' 'Ah'm the chairman of
the English Speak'n Oonion.'
Beecham said '*Who-ooo?*'
The voice repeated it.
'I *don't* believe it!' said Sir Thomas, replacing the
receiver.

On women

Asked whether it was true that he did not like women in the orchestra, Sir Thomas said: 'Well, I'm very fond of women, but in an orchestra if they're not good-looking —and often they're not and they always look worse when they're blowing—it puts me off, while if they *are* good-looking it puts me off a damn sight more.'

⚘

On another occasion:
'The trouble with women in an orchestra is that if they are attractive it will upset my players and if they're not it will upset me.'

⚘

'To women he referred once, saying that none was worth the loss of a night's sleep.'—Neville Cardus

Cup Final complexities

To his orchestra during a break in rehearsal: 'I am in a very awkward dilemma. I'd like a little advice. I went to the Cup Final, and before I went I indiscreetly let it be known that my sympathies were with Manchester United, and of course Bolton Wanderers won.

'On the day after the Cup I received a letter from Bolton reminding me that I was the chairman not only of the musical society but of the football club. . . . What do you do? How do you get out of that?'

Members of the orchestra: 'Resign! Abdicate!'

Sir Thomas: 'I think I'll say I divided my heart and mind—the intellectual and better part of me of course was with Bolton, and my compassionate sympathies were naturally with Manchester.'

♩

Beecham telephoned his solicitor, Philip Emanuel, and asked whether he might come round and watch the Cup Final on the television. Permission being granted, he arrived and spent a happy hour and a half cheering on one of the teams. Arriving back home, however, he telephoned again. It had just dawned on him, he said, that he had been consistently cheering on the wrong one.

𝄞

The last rehearsal with the Royal Philharmonic Orchestra at the Guildhall, Portsmouth, was held on Cup Final day. It had been in progress for only a short time when a giant television console was pushed on to the platform.

'Now, gentlemen,' said Sir Thomas, 'let's really get down to the most important business of the day—watching the match.'

Social and sociological

To a journalist who interviewed him on his return
from America while they were both being shaved in the
barber's shop at the Adelphi Hotel, Liverpool: 'I always
come to Liverpool for a shave. Do you?'
To which the interviewer replied in the same spirit:
'Invariably. I find it's the best place.'

§

Speaking of squatters who were occupying blocks of
flats in London because they could not find homes,
Beecham remarked: 'We're on their side, of course, but
we mustn't say so, must we?'

§

'Socially the Russians are unlike any other European
people, having a good deal of the Asiatic disregard for
the meaning and use of the hour-glass. Slow movement
and time without limit for reflection and conversation

73

are vital to them, and unless they can pass a substantial part of the day in discussions about the human soul they become ill at ease and unhappy.'

♩

At the Adelphi Hotel, Liverpool, one day it was hard to attract the attention of the wine waiter. This prompted Sir Thomas to tell how as a young man he had once waited for nearly twenty minutes without service at the Savoy Hotel in London. 'I stood on the table and clapped two plates together, and I have had wonderful service there ever since.'

♩

When Delius's opera *Koanga* was poorly supported in Liverpool, Sir Thomas exploded: 'This godforsaken city with not a decent theatre or concert-hall,* and a climate so evil that no self-respecting singer would set foot in it! It's a catarrhal place that has been the cause through centuries of the nasal Liverpool accent.'

♩

Nothing better in its line than Blackpool, said Sir Thomas, has ever been created.

---

* This was presumably before the new Philharmonic Hall was opened in 1939, when Beecham himself conducted the inaugural concerts.

On Hitler

When Sir Thomas met Hitler, the German dictator inquired: 'How do you think I would be received in your country?'

'You would, I have no doubt, be the object of great interest,' said Beecham.

Hitler said that if he came to London the matter of his safety would probably put a great strain on the police.

Beecham replied: 'You would be safer in London than in your own country.'

♩

Hitler, after expressing satisfaction that Sir Thomas had come to Germany with his orchestra, is reported to have said: 'I should have liked so much to come to London to participate in the Coronation festivities, but cannot risk putting the English to the inconvenience which my visit might entail.'

'Not at all,' replied Sir Thomas innocently. 'There

would be no inconvenience. In England we leave everybody to do exactly as he likes.'

Hitler is reported to have been nonplussed by this reply.

ʔ

To his orchestra in Berlin, when he observed Hitler applauding in his box: 'The old beggar seems to like it!'

This remark was heard throughout Europe over the radio. Beecham had seemingly forgotten that the concert was being broadcast.

ʔ

Asked what he thought of his meeting with Hitler, he replied: 'Now I know what's wrong with Germany.'

ʔ

When the LPO entertained the Berlin Philharmonic Orchestra in London before the last war, Sir Thomas told the Germans: 'When we were in Germany, at each town we visited a speech of welcome was made—each one identical. I also made a speech on each occasion— every one different. This will corroborate the well-known fact that things are so much better organised in your country than in ours.'

On 'Lollipops'

'A "lollipop" in accepted English terminology is a species of sweetmeat or candy. I have used the word in connection with music played by me in my concerts for the following reason. For many years past my audience at the close of a performance has had the disconcerting habit of remaining in its seats and declining to depart until, emulating Oliver Twist, it has obtained an extra helping. As in the majority of cases the usual programme ends with a grand bang or explosion of sound, my practice has been to play an encore which is in complete contrast.

'The piece selected has generally been of an essentially syrupy, soapy, soothing and even soporific nature, and the effect upon the audience has been that its emotional temperature, raised to a high point at the conclusion of the actual programme, is gradually reduced to the normal so that everyone walks out happy and comfortable.'

Jazz and film

Jazz: 'The most degraded form of human aberration.'

♩

'Many years ago a strange-looking man came to me and said: "Sir, we are going to put on the screen"—I don't think he said the screen; I think he called it the fillum—"on the fillum a private view of Goethe's *Faust* and music." A small room—I sat down, watched with amazement and listened with consternation.

'We came to the scene of Margaret and Faust in the garden. It occupied about 40 seconds. He said to me "This is where we must have the *Jool Song!*" I said "But it takes eight minutes for what you call the *Jool Song!*"

'And his face fell and he said, "Oh, couldn't we have a bit of it?" I then retired from the scene.'

♩

The Royal Philharmonic Orchestra was engaged to

perform the music for a film. The director wanted to run through the credit titles so that Beecham could work out the timing.

But Sir Thomas thought all this rather a waste of time. He looked impatiently at the long list of actors and technicians, then exclaimed: 'Who are all these nonentities?'

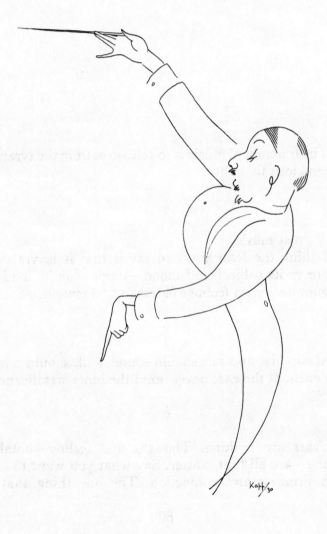

Thoughts on music and life

'The function of music is to release us from the tyranny of conscious thought.'

♩

Of great music:
'I think the least you can say is that it leaves you, whatever its subject and mood—tragic, comic, loud or languorous—with feelings of *wonder* and *contentment*.'

♩

'Music first and last should sound well, should allure and enchant the ear; never mind the inner significance.'

♩

'Years are nothing. Thought and feeling—notably feeling—are all that matter. Say what you want to say, with firmness and conviction. The one thing that is really important, in playing, in conducting—yes, and even in misconducting—is this: whatever you do, do it with conviction.'

ʔ

'I never think about the purists. They are a breed that has sprung up recently.'

ʔ

Of contemporary composers:
'No composer has written as much as a hundred bars of worth-while music since 1925. *Wozzeck* is ingenious, but uncivilised and uncharming. I am not interested in music—or in any work of art—that fails to stimulate enjoyment of life and, what is more, pride of life.'

ʔ

'Nobody has written a good tune for 30 years. No one has written a good opera since 1922.'

ʔ

'Festivals are for the purpose of attracting trade to the town. What that has to do with music I don't know.'

ʔ

'I sometimes wonder if I haven't wasted myself to some degree by giving myself almost wholly to music. For music does not ever encourage abstract thinking or pungency of comment or dialectical agility. Perhaps I was really born for the legal profession.'

Jeux d'esprit

Walking up Regent Street in his earlier years on a warm day, Beecham stopped a cab, placed his fur overcoat inside it, said to the driver 'Follow me about' and walked off.*

♩

Visited at Grosvenor House one morning by Alfred Francis, the director of the 1951 Liverpool Festival, and others, Beecham, sitting up in bed and smoking a cigar, declaimed against festivals (and music critics) for three-quarters of an hour and concluded: 'So it's no use your coming here to me and asking me to be your musical director as a distinguished musician.'

'But we're not asking you to be musical director as a distinguished musician,' he was told. 'We're asking you to conduct in Liverpool as a famous Lancastrian.'

* Strangely, there are Beecham admirers who get quite hot under the collar at this one, declaring it apocryphal or giving various other versions.

82

'Do you mean', said Beecham, calming down, 'as a freeman of St Helens?'

'Well,' said Francis, 'that kind of thing.'

'Your family', said Beecham, 'have been manufacturing confectionery in the North for about 200 years and my birthday happens to be at Easter.'

'Yes?' said the mystified Francis.

'It would be very appropriate if I received a Simnel cake and two dozen Eccles cakes,' said Beecham.

The deal was agreed and he conducted without fee in return for the cakes. The 'Easter' contract was kept up.

♩

Beecham had dined particularly well in a Northern hotel following a concert and afterwards could be seen making his way slowly up the winding staircase, removing the lamps from the holders at the side all the way up and dropping them into a tablecloth tucked into the waistband of his trousers.

On reaching the landing, he tipped the cloth and all its contents over the balustrade. The crash brought the night porters to the scene. Sir Thomas, looking down and waving his hand airily, cried 'Put it on my bill. Put it on my bill,' and proceeded on his way to bed.

♩

At a Christmas breakfast in New York Sir Thomas examined his Christmas tree, hung with gifts, then picked off a most gaudy tie and a bar of soap. 'That's for you, my boy,' he said, presenting both to the composer Richard Arnell.

♩

Asked by the young William Walton to look through the first draft of his oratorio *Belshazzar's Feast*, Sir

83

Thomas, after perusal, returned it with the words: 'This is a work which will never be heard, so I advise you to throw in all you can. Put in, for instance, a couple of brass bands for good and useless measure.'

Walton put in the additional brass and it proved a most effective idea.

♩

Beecham once announced that he was going to Lympne Castle, Sussex, for the final rehearsal of a play his sister had written—*Thomas Cranmer*.

'I am to play the principal part,' he said. 'But I have warned my sister that if I have not the time to learn it—then I shall improvise!'

♩

Sir Thomas said that after producing *The Faithful Shepherdess* by John Fletcher (1579–1625) he received a letter from the Inland Revenue asking for the address of Mr John Fletcher for the purposes of taxation, as they had been unable to discover his whereabouts.

'I was able to reply that to the best of my knowledge his present residence was the South Aisle of Southwark Cathedral and I went on to venture the opinion that he might find some difficulty in changing it.'

♩

At a concert the BBC were broadcasting Sir Thomas was to play the *Four Legends* of Sibelius. Only three, however, were at that moment available and the BBC insisted on a seven-minute filler. Beecham declared that this would unbalance the programme, but at last, to calm everyone, said 'Leave it to me.'

84

Just before playing the *Legends* he turned to the audience and started to explain the difficulty he was in, of choosing an appropriate filler for 'that august body, the BBC', fanatical about rigid timing. By the time he had cited several pieces he might have played and explained why each was unsuitable, and had chivvied the BBC a bit, it only remained to say: 'Oh, dear, I've been talking for seven minutes, so there won't be any necessity for the piece, will there?'

𝄞

Sir Thomas telephoned a South Kensington doctor he didn't know and requested him to come immediately. The doctor, flattered, arrived to find Beecham waiting in evening dress.

'No,' he said, 'I am not ill. But my car service has broken down and I'm due to conduct at the Albert Hall. As you live near it, would you be so kind as to motor me there? Here are two tickets for the performance.'

The doctor obliged and the tickets were cheerfully accepted.

𝄞

Asked by his father to alter some of the verses in the *Beecham's Pills Christmas Carol Annual* so as to advertise the business, Sir Thomas, after some meditation, produced the following:

> *Hark! the herald angels sing!*
> *Beecham's pills are just the thing.*
> *Two for a woman, one for a child . . .*
> *Peace on Earth and mercy mild!*

At eighty

On the eve of his eightieth birthday Sir Thomas was asked whether the standard of orchestral playing had improved since the beginning of his career. 'Oh, incontestably,' he replied. 'At the beginning of the century there was no standard to speak of.'

❡

At the lunch to celebrate his eightieth birthday: 'I just get the best players and let them play.... At rehearsal they play the piece through; any mistakes they know about as well as I do, so we play it through again; then they know it. And *I* know what they are going to do.... *They don't know what I am going to do* ... so that at the performance everyone is on his toes, and we get a fine performance.'

General

Sir Thomas's national anthems were magnificent and breath-taking. At a Hallé season in Manchester with his own orchestra his rendering of 'God Save the King', the *Manchester Guardian* reported, 'would have quelled a revolution.' His 'Star-Spangled Banner' in New York was said to have drawn delighted crowds to Carnegie Hall. And at a concert he gave in Paris the comment most frequently heard during the interval was an astonished 'Mais la Marseillaise!'

♩

When the London Philharmonic Orchestra was about to give a concert at the Paris Opéra in the thirties it was suddenly found that M. Lebrun, the French President, was coming. Curiously enough, there was no 'Marseillaise' in the Opéra music library and the baggage porter was sent out to scour the music shops. They were closed, but he procured from a back-street emporium a salon string orchestra arrangement.

With no time to spare, Beecham had the string parts copied and announced to the horns, trombones, percussion, etc.: 'I shall leave it to you gentlemen to improvise and improve in any way you think fit.'

The orchestra performed with brio, and perhaps this was the origin of Beecham's 'Marseillaise' that so delighted the French.

♩

Beecham told Neville Cardus of how he called at the Australian Broadcasting Authority and was received by a pretty girl in the outer office.

'To be approachable I said to her, "You are looking very handsome this morning, my dear." And she replied, "Ow, Sir Thomas, be your ha-ige." '

♩

Muriel Brunskill recalled that Sir Thomas and her husband, Robert Ainsworth the conductor, used to spend hours on free evenings during opera tours on two unexpected hobbies—the history and workings of ships and trains.

♩

Eric Fenby, acting temporarily as Beecham's secretary, and with his manservant on holiday, found Sir Thomas late one afternoon still in his underclothes, his bedroom in confusion. 'Master Fenby! Kindly extricate one complete outfit from amongst this debris! The trouble is: where are my bloody braces?'

After a frantic search, with a taxi at the door, Fenby, pulling the score of Chabrier's *España* from the bed, where Beecham had been studying it, discovered the inevitable red braces marking the irregular trombone entry.

♩

On one occasion Beecham's hostess brought out a record of Delius's *On Hearing the First Cuckoo in Spring* and put it on for him, saying that she had made heaps of Delius converts with it. He listened with patience, then mildly observed that it wasn't Delius at all, but Moszkowski's *Scherzo Capriccioso*. The labels had been transposed and the Delius was on the other side.

♩

There were times when Sir Thomas was short of money and once, planning a provincial tour, he was discussing staying with friends at some places; at others a hotel would be needed. An experienced friend then drew up a personal budget, which amounted to more than Beecham had anticipated. He turned to Lady Beecham (Betty Humby) and said, 'Who's going to ask your father, Betty, you or me?'

♩

Sir Thomas had returned to his hotel after conducting a concert in Manchester. In the foyer he saw a distinguished-looking woman whom he thought he knew, but he could not recollect her name.

As he passed, he stopped for a moment's conversation. Recalling vaguely that she had a brother and in the hope of thus identifying her, he inquired whether her brother was well and still doing the same job.

'Oh yes,' she replied. 'He is very well and is still King.'

'I was once, many years ago, taking part in a performance of *The Dream of Gerontius*—I don't very often do that sort of thing. You remember the place where there is a great crescendo and the tenor jumps up and says "Take me away"?

'It was already about a quarter to eleven and the heavy instruments had to go somewhere. At that moment four ruffianly-looking gentlemen rushed on to the platform, seized the big drum and the cymbals and disappeared.'

♩

Beecham enjoyed watching and hearing the comic band Robb Wilton used to conduct in his music-hall act, when the comedian would sometimes announce: 'Now I am going to play the Overture to "William T'Hell".'

Sir Thomas took over the joke and was known to declaim: 'Now for the Overture to "William T'Hell".'

♩

Arriving at Brussels, the LPO found that the basket containing all the music had been lost on the quay at Ostend. Some of the music was English and it was the first occasion on which a British subsidy had been obtained.

The Salle des Beaux Arts library produced Beethoven's Fifth Symphony, a Mendelssohn overture and a Haydn symphony, and the orchestra made do with these.

Beecham explained to the audience: 'At long last His Majesty's Government have recognised the existence of British music by supporting this visit to Brussels, but we are unfortunately unable to play any of it owing to an oversight on the part of the Belgian Railways.'

Beecham said he once bought a car, but after a time could not get it going. 'So I walked away and left the damned thing, and have no idea what became of it.'

This was said to have happened in the middle of Oxford Circus.

♩

There was a delay when the Royal party arrived late at the Edinburgh Festival performance of Beethoven's Ninth Symphony, and while waiting Beecham kept the four soloists in stitches of laughter by telling them stories.

When the Queen arrived he appeared a little mixed in his bows. He started to bow, as he always did, to the orchestra first, then broke off to start a bow to the audience, then broke that off to bow to the Queen.

It was the fastest performance of the Ninth Symphony, recalls Richard Arnell, that he ever heard.

♩

A trombone player made his debut one morning.

'You are new, aren't you?' said Beecham. 'What is your name?'

'Ball, sir.'

'How very singular,' observed Sir Thomas.

♩

When Beecham opened a new music library in Liverpool, the chairman introduced him in hearty style, saying: 'Sir Thomas, I need hardly say, is well known to us all. Many's the time we've been up to Philharmonic Hotel* to hear the band.'

* He meant Hall.

91

After the Promenade concert at Queen's Hall, conducted by Sir Henry Wood, on April 26th, 1940, when Beecham was abroad, the police asked the audience to stay because a heavy air raid was still on.

'. . . Ceremoniously the librarian distributed the parts for the *Figaro* Overture. The audience was amazed to see the living image of Sir Thomas Beecham with the well-trimmed beard walk, with the famous *maestoso* gait, to the rostrum . . . throwing away the score and disdainfully ordering the conductor's desk to be removed. . . . *And* the conductor found it necessary to shout "Shut up!" in the middle. The stretched-out arms and the baton, down-pointed in the familiar way for the *Figaro* opening, began to evoke something astonishingly like the world-famous Beecham interpretation! . . .

'The impersonator was Mr Ralph Nicholson, a young member of the London Symphony Orchestra's violin section.'

♩

The orchestra had gone on leave. Suddenly Beecham telephoned Eric Fenby from Sussex: 'I want an orchestra of 25! Recall the best players. Charing Cross 5 p.m. day after tomorrow, white ties, double pay. I must have Mr Beard and Mr Goossens! And I want the orchestration of some Grieg songs.'

Fenby could not get the parts from a hire library because of an outstanding account and had to orchestrate the songs himself, nor were the players happy at being recalled. The climax came, to Fenby's disgust, when Fred Lawrence, the orchestral manager, telephoned: 'What do you think? The blasted concert isn't till tomorrow night and the chaps haven't a tooth-brush between them!'

This was the end. Fenby tackled Sir Thomas furiously, to be told: 'Calm yourself. Calm yourself. I've put up Mr Beard in a cottage and Mr Goossens is comfortable in a windmill nearby!'

Fenby resigned on the spot and said he was leaving for Yorkshire. There he found a telegram awaiting him. 'Proceed to Paris. Select such material as you deem suitable for interpolation between the acts of *Koanga*. All expenses paid. Thomas Beecham.' So Fenby went to Paris and on his return Beecham said not a word about the incident.

At the rehearsal of *Koanga* Fenby mounted the Covent Garden podium and began 'Gentlemen. . . '. But that was as far as he got. There was a great roar of laughter from the orchestra.

♩

Sir Thomas had a tickle in his throat during a concert and was trying to suppress a cough. One of the front-desk players thoughtfully felt in his waistcoat pocket for a cough-drop and offered it to him.

Afterwards Beecham thanked the player, remarking that it had had a curious flavour.

'Well, Sir Thomas,' was the reply, 'It's been to the cleaners four times.'

♩

Arriving unexpectedly at one of his favourite Northern hotels, Sir Thomas was told that his usual room had been taken.

'I always have that room,' said Beecham. 'Couldn't you ask the occupant if he would transfer to another?'

'I think the gentleman has retired,' said the manager, doubtfully.

'I will go up and put it to him myself,' said Sir Thomas. He did so, accompanied by the manager. The other guest, aroused from his bed, replied 'Certainly not. I'll do nothing of the kind.'

'But', said the manager, 'this is Sir Thomas Beecham.'

The other man said, 'I don't care if it's Sir Malcolm Sargent.'

Acknowledgments

Acknowledgment is made to the following books by reference to page number followed by (in brackets) position number on the page:

The Orchestra Speaks, by Bernard Shore (Longmans, Green and Co. Ltd.), page 25(2, 3 and 4).

Sir Thomas Beecham, by Neville Cardus (William Collins Sons and Co. Ltd.), 45(1), 49(1), 50(3), 52(4 and 5), 53(1), 61(3), 67(1 and 3), 70(3), 80(4), 81(5), 85(3), 88(1).

Talking of Music, by Neville Cardus (William Collins Sons and Co. Ltd.), 14(1), 54(1), 67(4).

The Baton and the Jackboot, by Berta Geissmar (Hamish Hamilton Ltd., London, 1944), 14(4), 22(3), 39(3), 40(3), 45(2), 59(2), 63(1), 75(2), 92(1).

Sir Thomas Beecham, Conductor and Impresario, reissued as *Beecham Remembered* (Gerald Duckworth and Co. Ltd.), compiled and edited by Humphrey Procter-Gregg, 13(3), 14(2), 15(1, 4 and 5), 16(1), 17(1 and 2), 21(2 and 3), 24(2 and 4), 29(3), 31(3), 39(1), 40(1), 48(1), 50(2), 51(1), 55(3), 57(3), 68(2), 69(1), 74(1), 80(2), 81(2), 86(2), 88(2).

Thomas Beecham, by Charles Reid (Victor Gollancz Ltd.), 30(1), 33(1), 37(3), 40(2), 41(3), 45(4), 59(3), 62(1), 81(1), 86(1), 89(1).

A Mingled Chime, by Sir Thomas Beecham (Hutchinson Publishing Group Ltd.), 29(2), 46(1), 54(4), 55(1), 73(3).

Philharmonic, by Thomas Russell (Hutchinson Publishing Group Ltd.), 15(3), 64(1), 65(1).

The Great Conductors, by Harold C. Schonberg (Victor Gollancz Ltd.), 13(2), 17(3), 24(3), 31(1), 35(1), 43(1).
Also to:
The Beecham Society Newsletter, 44(2), 56(1).
EMI Ltd.: gramophone record, *Sir Thomas Beecham in Rehearsal* (Record 7 of HMV Haydn Box SLS 846), 19(2), 20(4), 23(3), 36(2), 46(2), 71(1), 78(2), 90(1).

Acknowledgment is made to the following for permission to reproduce photographs:
Radio Times Hulton Picture Library, for the Emu caricature, the Gordon Anthony portrait, and the photograph of Beecham rehearsing with the LPO; Godfrey MacDomnic, for the photograph of Beecham rehearsing with the RPO; EMI Ltd., for the photograph of Yehudi Menuhin with Beecham and Elgar; the *Evening News*, for the photograph of Beecham with Harold Atkins and John Pennington;

—and to the following for permission to reproduce illustrations in the text:

The Mansell Collection, for the caricature by Wayner on page 16 (from *Celebrities in Caricature*, 1931); Beacon Press of Boston, Mass., for the sketch by Olga Koussevitzky on page 26 (from *Gentlemen, more dolce please* by Harry Ellis Dickson, 1969); Edmond X. Kapp, for the drawings on pages 38 (1919) and 79 (1930—Collection Victoria and Albert Museum, London); Einar Nerman, for the caricature on page 47 (a similar version appeared in *The Tatler* in 1924); Mrs Geraldine Anderson, for the caricature by Edmund Dulac on page 58, depicting Beecham with Lady Cunard as Britannia (from *The Outlook*, 1919); Les Gibbard, for the caricature on page 94 (from the *Sunday Telegraph*, 1968).
The publishers express their thanks to Denham Ford and Allan Maund of the Beecham Society for their assistance in tracing some of the caricatures.